What jobs can a **digger** do?

3

dig

4

A digger can **dig**.

It **digs** a hole.

5

push

A digger
can **push**.

6

It **pushes**
the soil.

7

smash

8

A digger can **smash** walls.

It is very noisy!

9

grab

10

This digger can **grab**.

It **grabs** with its claw!

11

pick up

12 This digger **picks up** rocks.

It is very strong.

13

load

14

This digger **loads** a truck.

It works fast.

15

scoop

16 This digger **scoops** up rocks.

It has a big shovel.

17

drill

18

This digger **drills** a hole.

cut

This digger **cuts** down trees.

19

What can it do?

drill

load

push

grab

Match the words and pictures.

How many?

Can you count the diggers?

21

Can you dig?

dig

load

pick up

grab

22 What can you do like a digger?

Index

cut 19

dig 4

digger 2

drill 18

grab 10

load 14

pick up 12

push 6

scoop 16

smash 8

Can you find these
digger pictures in
the book?

23

For Parents and Teachers

Questions you could ask:

p. 2 What colour are these diggers? Yellow.
Diggers are usually painted a bright colour such as
orange/yellow so they are easily seen by workers.

p. 4 How does a digger dig? Point out the shovel
on this excavator and explain how it picks up soil,
turns and then drops the soil in a different place.

p. 5 How does this digger move? This digger,
called a bulldozer, moves on tracks. These help a
machine move over bumpy ground. Compare the
tracks with the wheels on page 8.

p. 8 Can you see the driver? The driver sits in the
cab. He turns around to operate the (pneumatic)
hammer/drill at the back of the machine.

p. 10 What is this digger doing? It is knocking
down an old house to make way for a new building.
The big claw tears down the walls.

p. 12 What makes a digger go? A digger needs a
strong engine to make it work. The engine on this
digger is at the back, behind the cab.

*p. 16 This digger is working in a mine. What is a
mine?* In a mine, rocks containing coal are dug
out of the ground. Other rocks may contain
metals such as gold or iron.

p. 18 How does a drill work? It spins around and
around to make a hole.

Activities you could do:

• Allow the reader to explore a selection of toys
which he/she can move by pulling, pushing,
turning handles, using appropriate vocabulary
such as "grab", "pick up", "push", "pull", "turn" etc.

• If you have a sand pit or visit a beach,
encourage the reader to use buckets, spades and
other tools to dig holes/build sandcastles etc.

• When you are out and about, look out for
building sites and diggers at work.

• Ask the reader to act out using tools, e.g. saw or
hammer, comparing these to jobs that diggers do.

• Introduce different building materials using the
nursery rhyme "London Bridge is Falling Down".

Paperback Edition 2009
© Aladdin Books Ltd 2006

Designed and produced by
Aladdin Books Ltd
PO Box 53987
London SW15 2SF

First published in 2006
by Franklin Watts
338 Euston Road
London NW1 3BH

Franklin Watts Australia
Level 17/207 Kent Street
Sydney NSW 2000

Franklin Watts is a division of
Hachette Children's Books, an
Hachette Livre UK company.
www.hachettelivre.co.uk

ISBN 978 0 7496 8974 2

A catalogue record for
this book is available
from the British Library.

Dewey Classification: 629.225

Printed in Malaysia
Series consultant
Zoe Stillwell is an experienced
Early Years teacher currently
teaching at Pewley Down Infant
School, Guildford.

Photocredits:
*l-left, r-right, b-bottom, t-top,
c-centre, m-middle*
All photos courtesy John Deere
except: 2-3 — Photodisc. 4-5, 12-13,
23tl & mbr — courtesy Caterpillar.
10-11, 20tl, 21, 22tl, 23bl — Select
Pictures. 16-17, 23tr — Corbis. 22tr &
br — Comstock. 22bl — TongRo.